THE LITTLE BOOK OF
DINOSAURS

Linda Sonntag

www.alligatorbooks.co.uk

The Alligator logo is a registered trade mark of
Alligator Books Ltd.

Published by Alligator Books Ltd
Gadd House, Arcadia Avenue
London N3 2JU

Printed in China

Contents

KING DINO

Tyrannosaurus rex **is one of the most famous dinosaurs.**

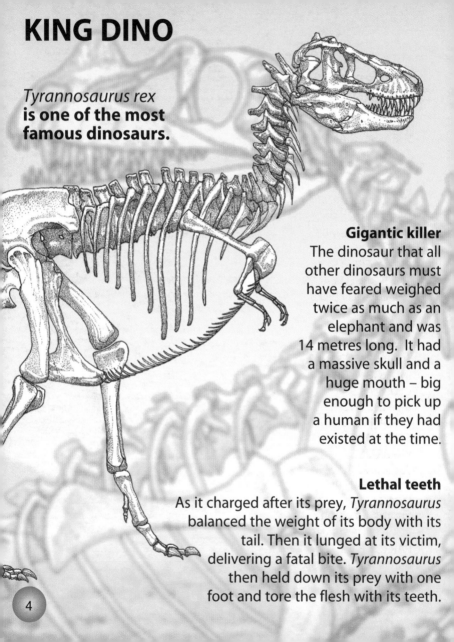

Gigantic killer

The dinosaur that all other dinosaurs must have feared weighed twice as much as an elephant and was 14 metres long. It had a massive skull and a huge mouth – big enough to pick up a human if they had existed at the time.

Lethal teeth

As it charged after its prey, *Tyrannosaurus* balanced the weight of its body with its tail. Then it lunged at its victim, delivering a fatal bite. *Tyrannosaurus* then held down its prey with one foot and tore the flesh with its teeth.

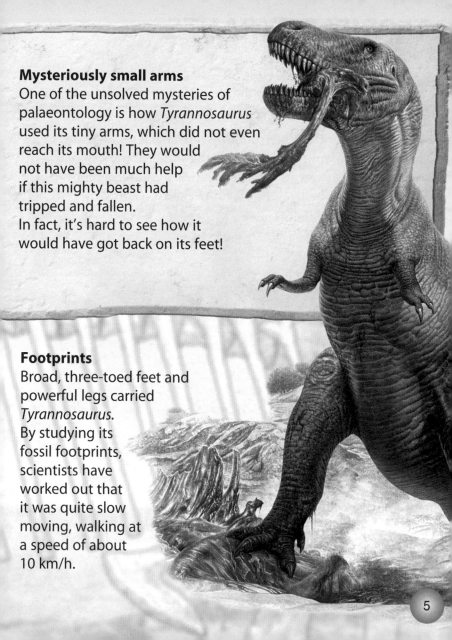

Mysteriously small arms

One of the unsolved mysteries of palaeontology is how *Tyrannosaurus* used its tiny arms, which did not even reach its mouth! They would not have been much help if this mighty beast had tripped and fallen. In fact, it's hard to see how it would have got back on its feet!

Footprints

Broad, three-toed feet and powerful legs carried *Tyrannosaurus*. By studying its fossil footprints, scientists have worked out that it was quite slow moving, walking at a speed of about 10 km/h.

TERRIBLE TYRANTS

Jaws
Albertosaurus and *Daspletosaurus* were smaller and faster than their terrifying cousin *Tyrannosaurus*, but they all had the same huge jaws and sharp, backward-pointing teeth. *Daspletosaurus* (below left) may have killed its prey by biting into the animal's flanks and letting it bleed to death.

Neck attack
Albertosaurus (below right) was 9 metres long and weighed about 3 tonnes. It takes its name from Alberta, Canada, where it was first discovered in 1892. *Albertosaurus* probably ambushed or chased after its prey, then killed it by biting a lump of flesh from its neck.

Angry diners
Albertosaurus and the other tyrannosaurids probably fought when killing or scavenging beasts that were already dead.

JURASSIC GIANTS

The Jurassic Period began about 195 million years ago when the giant theropods (meat-eating dinosaurs) first walked the Earth.

Scavenger
Dilophosaurus (below left) was one of the first large meat-eaters. It appeared about 190 million years ago. The 6 metre long beast had more delicate jaws than its later relatives, and may have fed more by scavenging than killing.

Bony bumps
Ceratosaurus (centre) lived at the same time as *Allosaurus* (far right), but was half its size and fed on smaller prey. Its name means horned reptile, and was chosen because of the bony bumps on its skull.

Most common killer

The best-known Jurassic theropod was *Allosaurus* (below right). This 12 metre long giant lived about 150 million years ago. It was first discovered in 1877 in Colorado, USA. Later, 5,000 *Allosaurus* bones were found in a quarry in Utah, USA. It is believed to have been the most abundant meat-eater of its day.

Allosaurus killed by clamping its jaws around the neck of its victim. Its powerful teeth then tore the flesh of its prey into huge chunks.

TALL AND VEGGIE

The first *Plateosaurus* specimens were found in 1837 in Germany. Later, masses of complete *Plateosaurus* skeletons and single bones were found at the same site.

Drowned in a desert
Plateosaurus has been found in France and Switzerland as well as Germany. Scientists believe that large herds may have drowned in a freak flood while migrating across the desert that covered the area at the time.

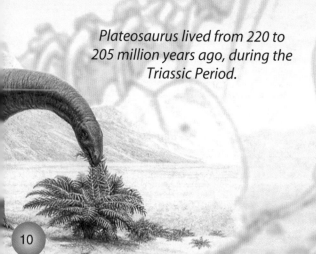

Plateosaurus lived from 220 to 205 million years ago, during the Triassic Period.

Lumbering browser

Plateosaurus was a Triassic giant that grew up to 8 metres long and weighed about 6 tonnes. *Plateosaurus* used its huge, clawed hands to pull fern fronds into its mouth. It may also have used its largest thumb claw for fighting off predators.

Prosauropod

Plateosaurus was the first large prosauropod (before sauropod). Over millions of years prosauropod relatives evolved into the giant sauropods of the Jurassic Period, such as *Diplodocus*.

LONGEST EVER

The sauropods were plant-eating dinosaurs – herbivores. They had small heads and extremely long necks, which they could swing to and fro.

The biggest dinosaurs

The sauropods were the giants of the Jurassic Period. They lived 160 to 150 million years ago, and were the longest, tallest and heaviest creatures ever to walk the Earth. The only animal bigger than them is the blue whale, which weighs up to 200 tonnes.

Diplodocus (below, left) was one of the longest of the sauropods, measuring 27 metres from snout to tail. Apatosaurus (right) was smaller, at 21 metres, but weighed a massive 30 tonnes!

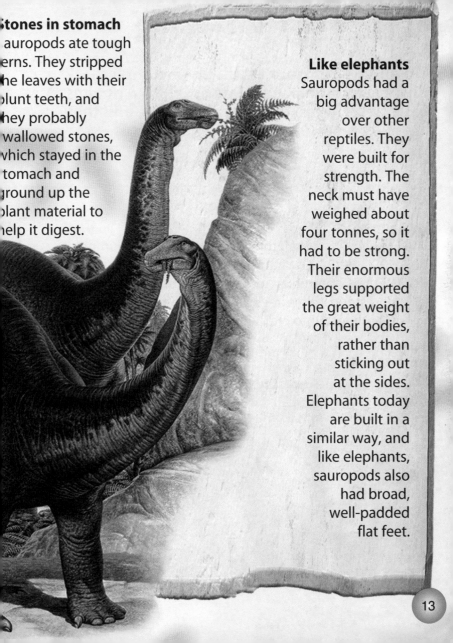

Stones in stomach
Sauropods ate tough ferns. They stripped the leaves with their blunt teeth, and they probably swallowed stones, which stayed in the stomach and ground up the plant material to help it digest.

Like elephants
Sauropods had a big advantage over other reptiles. They were built for strength. The neck must have weighed about four tonnes, so it had to be strong. Their enormous legs supported the great weight of their bodies, rather than sticking out at the sides. Elephants today are built in a similar way, and like elephants, sauropods also had broad, well-padded flat feet.

MIGHTIEST MONSTER

Most huge dinosaur fossils are incomplete. However, complete skeletons of *Brachiosaurus* have been found in Tanzania, Africa, and they are truly monumental.

Museum piece

One *Brachiosaurus* skeleton is on display at the Humboldt Museum in Berlin, Germany, where it towers four storeys high! With its enormous front legs and long neck, this sauropod stood 12 metres tall and could reach far above any other dinosaur to crop the leaves of the tallest trees.

First find

The first *Brachiosaurus* was found in Colorado, USA, in 1900. It was 22.5 metres long and weighed a massive 50 tonnes. It had a crest above its eyes, and blunt, peg-like teeth.

As big as six elephants
Bones of *Camarasaurus* were first discovered in Colorado in 1877. At 18 metres long, it was much smaller than its relative *Brachiosaurus*, but it was still the size of six elephants, and its leg bones were as thick as tree trunks!

Long stay
These creatures first appeared in early Jurassic times, about 185 million years ago, and survived until the end of the dinosaur era.

Camarasaurus (below far right) had a short snout and sharp snipping teeth.

CLAWS AND SCALES

The sauropods survived attacks from predators from the early Jurassic Period until the late Cretaceous Period, when dinosaurs disappeared from the Earth.

Volcano tooth

Vulcanodon (right) is known from just one incomplete skeleton found in Zimbabwe, Africa. Its name means 'volcano tooth' – the first fossil was a tooth found near some ancient volcanic lava.

Killer claw

At 6.5 metres long, *Vulcanodon* was a small sauropod. Its toes ended in hooves, except for the thumb, which had a sharp claw, possibly for fighting off predators.

Armour plating

By the late Cretaceous Period, most sauropods were armoured with plates. The plates made it much more difficult for predators (such as *Tyrannosaurus)* to kill them for food.

Chain mail

The 12 metre long *Saltasaurus* (right) lived about 70 million years ago in present-day Argentina. It had bony plates of various sizes set in its skin. These joined up to form an armour-like chain mail. When feeding, its strong tail was used as a prop so that it could lift its front quarters off the ground. Its tail was probably also used as a weapon.

INCREDIBLE STRENGTH

The skeleton of a sauropod was built for strength rather than for speed.

Underwater theory

The picture below shows a sauropod, *Brachiosaurus,* standing in deep water. At one time scientists believed that *Brachiosaurus* lived underwater – the water helping to support the great weight of its body (as it does with us if we go swimming). But *Brachiosaurus* could not have breathed underwater, because its lungs would have been 5 metres below the surface. At that depth, the water pressure would have squashed the lungs.

Mighty neck muscles

A large sauropod's neck weighed about 4 tonnes, so it needed powerful muscles to move it about as the beast browsed the leaves of tall trees. The sauropod's tail was like a mighty whip. The beast would raise it and swing it from side to side to whack its predators.

Lethal kick

If a sauropod was attacked from the front, it could rear up onto its hind legs, using its tail as a support, and deliver a fatal kick to its enemy. Once the enemy was on the ground, all the sauropod had to do was stamp on it to crush the breath out of it.

DAGGER THUMBS

The ornithopods (bird-footed dinosaurs) had huge hind feet with three toes. Each toe ended in a small hoof. But their powerful hands were armed with dagger-like claws on the thumbs, which they used for attacking enemies.

Campto-saurus
It's name means 'bent lizard'. This dino grew up to 7 metres long and weighed about one tonne.

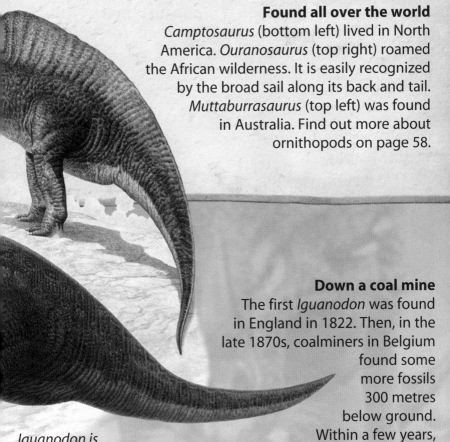

Found all over the world

Camptosaurus (bottom left) lived in North America. *Ouranosaurus* (top right) roamed the African wilderness. It is easily recognized by the broad sail along its back and tail. *Muttaburrasaurus* (top left) was found in Australia. Find out more about ornithopods on page 58.

Down a coal mine

The first *Iguanodon* was found in England in 1822. Then, in the late 1870s, coalminers in Belgium found some more fossils 300 metres below ground. Within a few years, scientists had recovered more than 39 *Iguanodon* skeletons from the mine, many of them complete.

Iguanodon is the best-known ornithopod. It lived in the Cretaceous Period, about 130 million years ago.

DUCKBILLS

Hadrosaurs, or duckbilled dinosaurs, had a wide, flat, toothless, duck-like beak for ripping off plant food.

Kritosaurus
Kritosaurus (near right) had a low crest over its snout. Scientists think it was covered with loose skin that blew up like a balloon when the creature bellowed.

Big feet
Duckbills first appeared about 100 million years ago in Asia and North America (when it was one landmass). *Edmontosaurus* (front) was one of the largest. It could run on two or four feet.

Distinctive head shapes
Hadrosaurs had similar skeletons, but different-shaped heads. *Bactrosaurus* (top) was one of the earliest hadrosaurs and had a short snout. *Anatotitan* (below right) had a long snout and a prominent duckbill.

Lots of teeth
At the backs of their mouths, duckbills had row upon row of closely packed teeth that ground twigs, fruits and seeds to a pulp ready for swallowing.

CRAZY CRESTS

Hadrosaurs had some of the strangest heads of all dinosaurs. Each species of Hadrosaur had a unique crest shape that made its own sound.

Dino snorkels?

Even more amazing than duckbills were the dinosaurs' fantastic crests. Scientists once thought the crests were used like snorkels for underwater breathing. But this was not possible as they had no openings at the top.

Inflatable skin

Saurolophus (bottom left) had a short, solid crest at the base of its skull. This may have supported a bag of skin that it could inflate when bellowing.

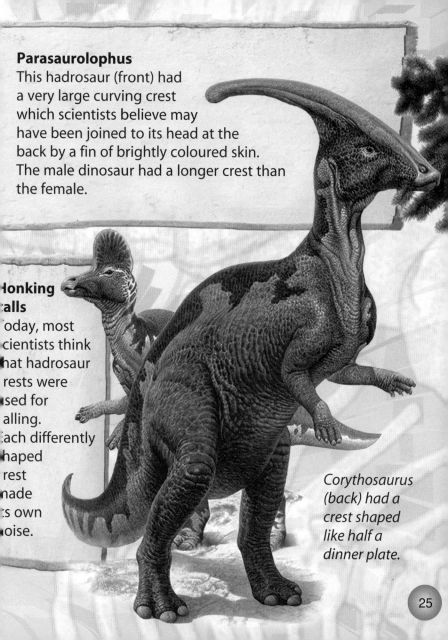

Parasaurolophus
This hadrosaur (front) had
a very large curving crest
which scientists believe may
have been joined to its head at the
back by a fin of brightly coloured skin.
The male dinosaur had a longer crest than
the female.

**Honking
calls**
Today, most
scientists think
that hadrosaur
crests were
used for
calling.
Each differently
shaped
crest
made
its own
noise.

*Corythosaurus
(back) had a
crest shaped
like half a
dinner plate.*

25

Plentiful and widespread

Hadrosaurs were some of the last dinosaurs to walk the Earth. They first appeared about 100 million years ago in eastern Asia and western North America (which were joined at the time). At some sites in Mongolia, hundreds of skeletons have been found together.

Slow mover

Hadrosaurs were huge, weighing between 5 and 10 tonnes. They moved slowly on all-fours, munching on plants with their sharp duckbills. When ambushed by an enemy, they could rear up and run away on their hind legs, holding their long tails straight out behind.

Honker

Parasaurolophus had a crest that was more than twice the length of its skull. Air tubes from the nostrils ran inside the crest. As the creature breathed, it probably made a loud honking noise through its nose. The male had a longer crest than the female.

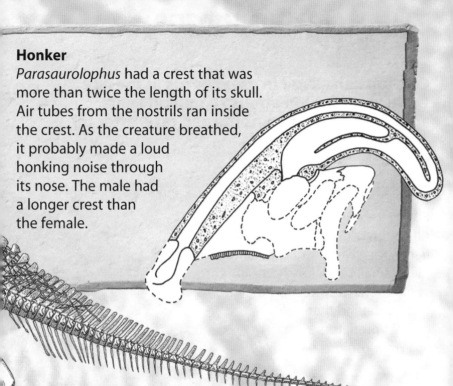

Claws and hooves

Although the crests of hadrosaurs were very different, their powerfully built skeletons were similar. Hadrosaur bodies were well adapted for running fast over short distances to escape predators. Some of the fingers on their hands ended in claws, but others ended in hooves, which suggests they were used for walking as well as for gripping.

THE HORNED FACES

Ceratopsians lived in great herds in the late Cretaceous Period about 70 million years ago. Their name means horned face, after the armoury on their heads.

Fierce veggies
Although ceratopsians looked extremely fierce, they were actually plant-eaters with many small teeth for chomping through vegetation. They needed their horns and frills to defend themselves against predators such as *Tyrannosaurus*.

Centrosaurus
The Ceratopsian had a single horn on its nose and a neck frill formed from a circular rim of bone, edged in spikes. Two sharp horns curled down over the top of the frill.

What a frill

At the back of its head *Triceratops* had a long neck shield, called a frill, made of bone and covered in tough hide. Around the edge were bony studs. This protected the dinosaur's fleshy neck from the teeth and claws of its enemies.

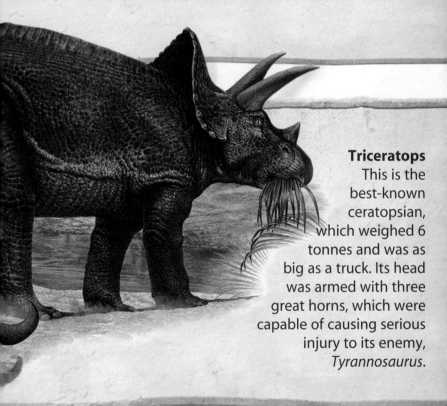

Triceratops
This is the best-known ceratopsian, which weighed 6 tonnes and was as big as a truck. Its head was armed with three great horns, which were capable of causing serious injury to its enemy, *Tyrannosaurus*.

SPIKES AND FRILLS

The ceratopsians had huge neck shields, known as frills. Their frills and horns were massively heavy and must have slowed the beasts down as they lumbered about.

Wrestling match
A male ceratopsian's head armoury wasn't just for defence. In the mating season, males were thought to have locked horns and wrestled against each other for females.

Muscle power
The ceratopsians' jaw muscles were attached to their bony frills, giving the jaws enormous power. The frills themselves may have been brightly coloured, and used for signalling to the herd.

Pentaceratops (top) means five-horned face. This fearsome beast actually had three horns, plus two pointed cheekbones beneath its eyes, as well as a huge frill edged with spikes.

Anchiceratops (centre) had long, pointed horns over its eyes and a huge neck frill with a row of sharp horns at its crest.

Torosaurus
This dinosaur (bottom) had head and neck frills that were 3.5 metres long – the same length as an average family car, and half the length of the whole animal. This massive plant-eating beast weighed 6 tonnes. It was first discovered in 1891 in Wyoming, USA.

BIG HEADS

All ceratopsians had similar skeletons, but the horns and frills were different in each species.

Huge body

Ceratopsians had strongly built skeletons to carry the enormous weight of their bodies and huge heads – the biggest were four or five times bigger than a rhinoceros. Their legs were stout pillars, like an elephant's, but much bigger. Ceratopsians may look fierce, but they were in fact plant-eaters.

Headache

The ceratopsians' massive heads were mostly bone and muscle, with only small brains. If the frill of *Chasmosaurus* (below) had been solid bone, it would not have been able to lift its head off the ground! Turn to page 62 to find out about another, quite different ceratopsian.

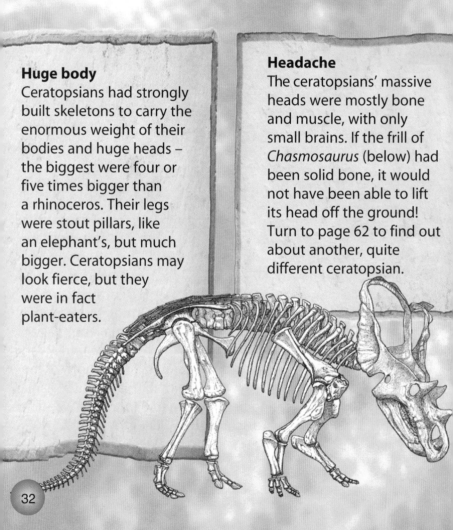

Defence tactics

Because of its weight, a ceratopsian was not able to run fast. When danger threatened, it stood still and faced the enemy with lowered head. All but the fiercest predators would have been frightened away. A threatened herd probably formed a circle around its young to shield them from attack. Not even *Tyrannosaurus* could have killed a ceratopsian without getting badly injured.

HEADBUTTERS

Pachycephalosaurs were strange-looking dinosaurs with dome-shaped heads and bird-like feet.

Whose teeth?

The first fossils of a pachycephalosaur ever found were some teeth. They were dug up in the 1850s, but scientists were unable to work out which dinosaur they belonged to. Then, in 1924, a skull and skeleton of the *Stegoceras* were found.

Safety helmet

Stegoceras (bottom) was unlike any other dinosaur previously found. It had a head like a safety helmet. The group name pachycephalosaur, means 'thick-headed reptile'.

Lost and found
Pachycephalosaurus (centre) was 8 metres long. Only its skull and a few bone fragments have been found so far. The huge thickness of its skull made it preserve more easily as a fossil.

Thick-head!
The skull bones of *Pachycephalosaurus* were of normal thickness for a dinosaur. But the bones on the roof of its head were an astonishing 22 cm thick!

Hard helmets
Rival males probably headbutted each other in fighting rituals to win females. The thicker the skull, the more chance of winning.

DOUBLE TROUBLE

Stegosaurus **(far right) is an unmistakable dinosaur because of the spectacular double row of plates running down its back. The plates were not fixed to its skeleton, and probably stood up like gigantic leaves – but what were they for?**

Central heating

Some scientists believe the plates were covered in a network of blood vessels under a layer of tough skin. The dinosaur could have turned its plates to the Sun to get warm in the morning; or perhaps the plates were covered with horn and were used to protect the backbone from the jaws of meat-eaters like *Allosaurus*.

Family ties

Stegosaurus's relatives were *Tuojiangosaurus* (left) and *Kentrosaurus*. *Tuojiangosaurus* was 6 metres long with cone-shaped plates arranged like a fence along its back. Turn to page 39 to learn about *Kentrosaurus*.

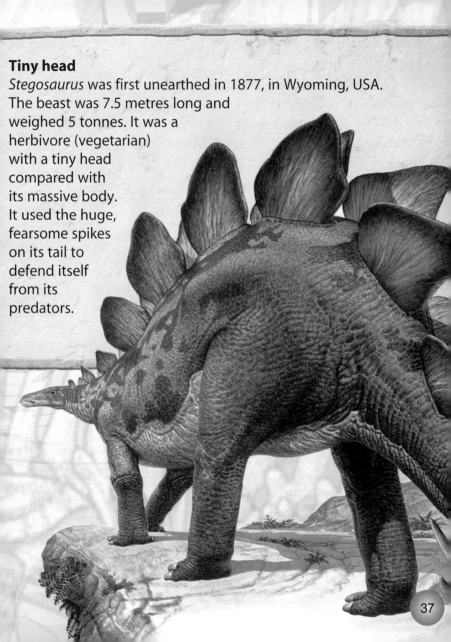

Tiny head

Stegosaurus was first unearthed in 1877, in Wyoming, USA. The beast was 7.5 metres long and weighed 5 tonnes. It was a herbivore (vegetarian) with a tiny head compared with its massive body. It used the huge, fearsome spikes on its tail to defend itself from its predators.

SCARY SKELETON

Stegosaurs were built with massive legs to support their huge weight. Their front legs were half the length of their back legs, so it would have been impossible for them to run fast.

Small brain
The narrow skull of *Stegosaurus* had a tiny space for a brain. The brain was about the size of a walnut, so it was not very intelligent!

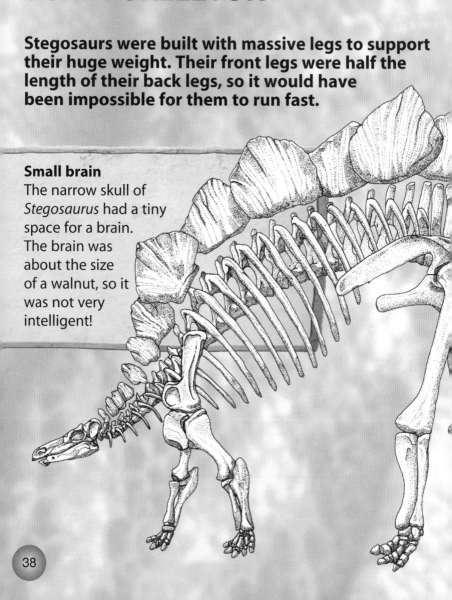

Kentrosaurus

At only 2.5 metres long, *Kentrosaurus* was the smallest of the stegosaur family. It had narrow plates and spikes down its back which may have also covered its hips and shoulders. It also had a pair of spines above its legs.

Elephant toes

Stegosaurs had sturdy, elephant-like feet with rounded claws. It had five toes on the front feet and four on the back.

Fossilized remains

Kentrosaurus, like the other stegosaurs, lived between 150 and 140 million years ago. Its fossilized remains have been found only in Tanzania, Africa.

INDESTRUCTIBLE

Ankylosaurs had an amazing suit of bony armour that made them almost indestructible.

Lumbering tanks

These great tank-like beasts lived towards the end of the dinosaur era during the Cretaceous Period. They lumbered about on all-fours, feeding on plants by slicing them off with their horny beaks.

Bony plates

Like all herbivores, ankylosaurs needed good defence. Their bodies were clad in thick bony plates and armed with fearsome spikes. If *Tyrannosaurus* had tried to attack one, it would have broken its teeth on the armour plating, or been gashed by the horns.

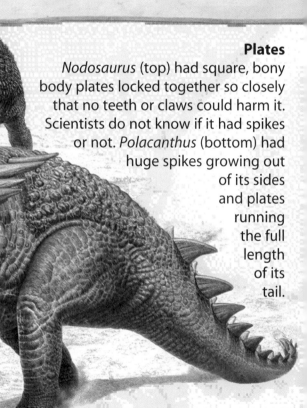

Third to be discovered

The bones of *Hylaeosaurus* (far left) were first dug up in England in 1833 – it was the third dinosaur ever discovered! From its incomplete remains, paleontologists worked out that the beast was 4 metres long and weighed 1 tonne.

Plates

Nodosaurus (top) had square, bony body plates locked together so closely that no teeth or claws could harm it. Scientists do not know if it had spikes or not. *Polacanthus* (bottom) had huge spikes growing out of its sides and plates running the full length of its tail.

CLUB TAILS

In addition to bony plated armour and fearsome spikes, some ankylosaurs had massive clubs on their tails.

Heavy amour
Pinacosaurus (below) and *Euoplocephalus* (right) were built like huge tanks. They roamed the Earth in the late Cretaceous Period. If an enemy attacked, these mighty beasts crouched on all-fours and relied on their heavy armour to protect them. They could knock a predator senseless with a blow from their clubbed tails.

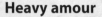

Pinacosaurus was discovered in the Gobi Desert in Mongolia, Central Asia. Its huge tail club was made of solid bone. A blow from it would have smashed the skull of a predator, like Velociraptor.

Clubbed tails

Euoplocephalus, discovered in 1902 in Alberta, Canada, weighed about 2 tonnes and measured 6 metres long. As well as having a massive tail club, it had an extra layer of bony plates on its head and back, and horns on its head, shoulders and arms. Their clubbed tails were strong and could make accurate blows when defence was required.

Harmless vegetarians!

The fearsome ankylosaurs were herbivores (plant-eaters). They had horny beaks for slicing off ferns and twigs, and small, leaf-shaped teeth for chewing. They needed to eat a lot of plant material each day to keep themselves full and to survive.

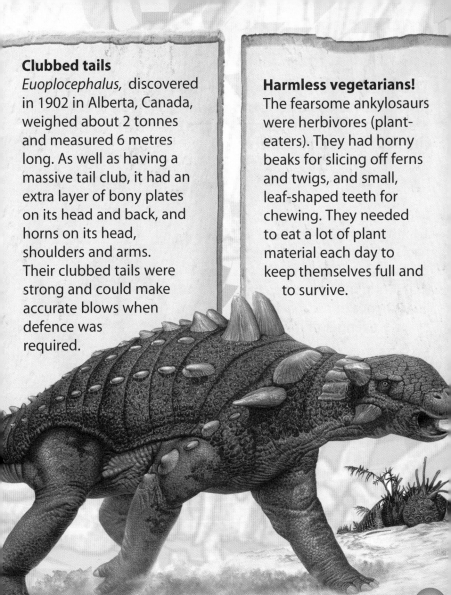

MEAT-MUNCHERS

The meat-eating theropods weren't all huge monster killers like *Tyrannosaurus*. **There were also many small theropods that needed to be fierce hunters to survive.**

Scavenger

The theropod *Ornitholestes* had strong jaws lined with sharp, backwards-pointing teeth. Any prey that it gripped with these had little chance of escape. It was also a scavenger of dead carcasses.

Nimble-toed

The small theropods were built for speed. Their hind legs were long and slender, and they walked and ran on their toes like birds. This left their hands free to snatch up prey. Their strong tails acted as rudders as they dashed along, and provided balance when they stood at rest.

Coelophysis
Coelophysis (below left) lived in North America about 225 million years ago. It was about 3 metres long and stood 1.5 metres tall. In 1947, paleontologists in New Mexico, USA, found whole herds of the beasts that had probably died of thirst as they roamed the land in search of water.

Tiny hunter
Compsognathus (above right) was one of the smallest dinosaurs ever it – was less than 1 metre long. It chased after small lizards and tasty insects.

LIKE AN OSTRICH!

**During the Late Cretaceous Period, a group
of dinosaurs called ornithomimids, or ostrich
dinosaurs, roamed the Earth. Like ostriches,
they had long, slender hind legs and long necks.**

Balance
When running at
full speed, the
ornithomimid
Dromiceiomimus
tucked its arms up
under its chest and
stuck out its fleshy
tail to act as a
counterbalance
as a kangaroo
does today.

Vicious beaks
Ornithomimids had powerful fingers and sharp claws for
grabbing prey or branches. But they had no teeth. Their
beaks must have been razor-edged for tearing flesh and
shearing leaves.

Dino racer
Struthiomimus (below right) could have run at up to 50 km/h which is as fast as a racehorse. It was certainly fast enough to catch a tasty dragonfly on the wing.

A *Struthiomimus* was up to 4 metres long and weighed 100 kg. Paleontologists first unearthed its skeleton in 1917, in Alberta, Canada.

Good mother
Oviraptoroids, such as *Oviraptor* (centre), were relatives of the ostrich dinosaurs. *Oviraptor* was given its name, which means 'egg thief', because it was first found near nests, in Mongolia. But it was later shown that it was looking after its own eggs, not stealing someone else's!

FAST AND FIERCE

Take-away food

The skeleton of only one *Segisaurus* (below) has ever been found. It was discovered in Arizona, USA. This small, fast-moving theropod had short arms, with three fingers on each hand. It used its hands for carrying pieces of flesh away from the kill, so it could eat them alone in safety.

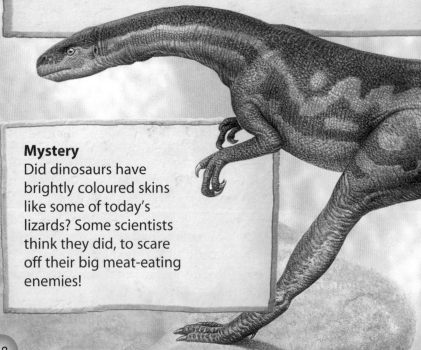

Mystery

Did dinosaurs have brightly coloured skins like some of today's lizards? Some scientists think they did, to scare off their big meat-eating enemies!

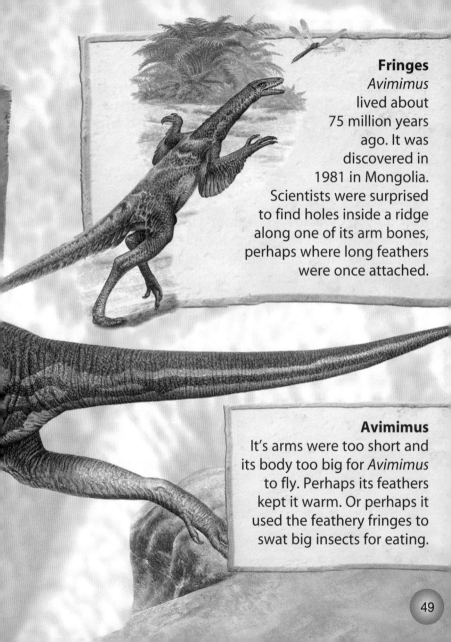

Fringes
Avimimus lived about 75 million years ago. It was discovered in 1981 in Mongolia. Scientists were surprised to find holes inside a ridge along one of its arm bones, perhaps where long feathers were once attached.

Avimimus
It's arms were too short and its body too big for *Avimimus* to fly. Perhaps its feathers kept it warm. Or perhaps it used the feathery fringes to swat big insects for eating.

49

BIG BRAINS

Dinosaurs were not the most intelligent beasts. But one group, the troodontids, was much cleverer than the rest. They had big brains and big eyes.

How do you measure a dinosaur's intelligence?

The bigger the brain a creature has, the more intelligent it is. You can tell how big a dinosaur's brain was by filling the brain cavity in its skull with sand, then tipping the sand into a measuring jug. For their body size, troodontid brains were two or three times bigger than normal-sized dinosaur brains.

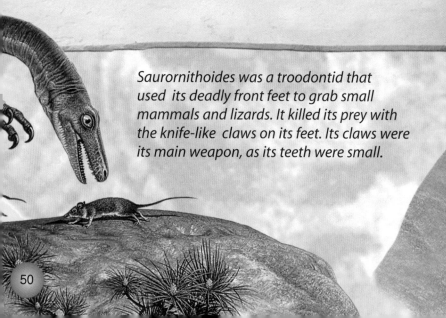

Saurornithoides was a troodontid that used its deadly front feet to grab small mammals and lizards. It killed its prey with the knife-like claws on its feet. Its claws were its main weapon, as its teeth were small.

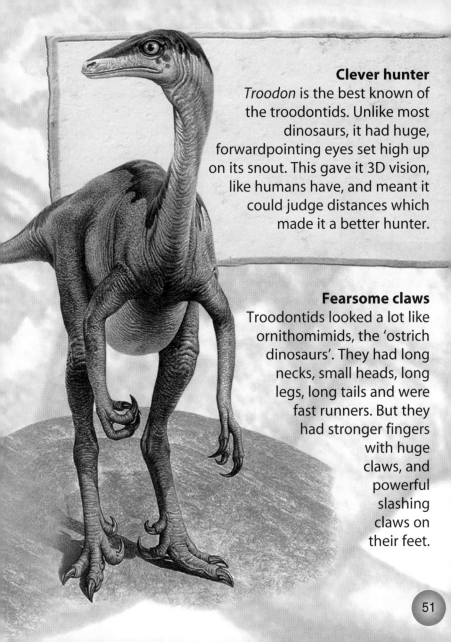

Clever hunter

Troodon is the best known of the troodontids. Unlike most dinosaurs, it had huge, forwardpointing eyes set high up on its snout. This gave it 3D vision, like humans have, and meant it could judge distances which made it a better hunter.

Fearsome claws

Troodontids looked a lot like ornithomimids, the 'ostrich dinosaurs'. They had long necks, small heads, long legs, long tails and were fast runners. But they had stronger fingers with huge claws, and powerful slashing claws on their feet.

SLASHING CLAWS

The most fearsome killers in the dinosaur world were the dromaeosaurids. They were only as tall as a human, but were intelligent and had good eyesight. They also had a huge slashing claw on each foot.

Secret weapon

About 100 years ago, incomplete skeletons of the first dromaeosaurid, *Dromaeosaurus* (front), were found.

Then, in 1964, whole skeletons of a new dromaeosaurid, *Deinonychus* (back) were found in the USA. Scientists were amazed to see it had a huge claw 10 times bigger than its other claws on its second toe.

Grip and rip

Deinonychus had strong jaws lined with many backwards pointing teeth, which it used for gripping prey. With its prey firmly held, it stood on one leg and probably ripped a 1 metre gash in the animal's flesh with its slasher claws. Find out more on the next page.

Fossilized fight

Velociraptor (right) is a well known dromaeosaurid. It was a relative of *Deinonychus*, although *Velociraptor* was half the size of *Deinonychus*. *Velociraptor* could run at over 35 km/h. In Mongolia, an astonishing fossil was found of it locked in combat with a horned dinosaur named *Protoceratops*.

PACK HUNTERS

Deinonychus **was the perfect hunter. Its streamlined body was fully developed for speed and attack, and it had strong jaw muscles for gripping and tearing flesh. But the dinosaur's main weapon was its great slashing claws.**

Attack from behind
When hunting a small dinosaur, *Deinonychus* chased its prey from behind until it could grab it and bring it down.

In for the kill
Deinonychus leapt on the back of its prey and sunk its teeth into the victim's neck.

Ganging up

When chasing its prey, *Deinonychus* pelted along with its slasher claws held upright. It probably hunted larger dinosaurs in a pack. *Tenontosaurus*, for example, was 10 times bigger than *Deinonychus*, but it didn't stand a chance if chased by several of the small predators.

Fatal cut

As its victim fell to the ground, *Deinonychus* leapt on to its belly and slashed its flesh open with its killer claw. At the same time it had to look out and listen for danger. Then the feast could begin.

DOG-SIZED DINO

Many small dinosaurs were vegetarians. Among the first plant-eaters to appear on Earth were the prosauropods of the Late Triassic Period. They lived about 210 million years ago.

Plant shredder

One of the smallest prosauropods was *Anchisaurus*. It had a small head, a long neck and a relatively big body, which suggests it was a vegetarian (plant-eaters need a bigger gut than meat-eaters). It also had small, blunt, tightly packed teeth ideal for shredding plants. Standing on its hind legs, it probably cut branches using the claws on its thumbs.

Powerful tail

Anchisaurus skeletons have deep, rib-like bones along the tail. This means the tail was full of muscles and very powerful. *Anchisaurus* probably slashed its tail from side to side to scare off predators.

First US dino bones

Fossils of *Anchisaurus* were the very first dinosaur remains to be found in North America. The bones were dug up in 1818 in Connecticut, eastern USA. At the time, no one knew what they were.

Balancing act

Anchisaurus was no taller than a terrier dog, but much longer. It walked on all-fours, but it could run at speed on just its hind legs, using its long tail for balance.

VEGGIE ARMOUR

The main group of vegetarian dinosaurs was called the ornithopods. Since plant-eaters were always prey to meat-eaters, ornithopods needed good defence tactics. Some developed hard, scaly skins and strong legs for running.

Cat-sized dino
The first ornithopods lived in the late Triassic and Early Jurassic Periods, about 200 million years ago. *Lesothosaurus* (top left) was discovered in Lesotho, southern Africa, in 1964. It was only 90 cm long (hardly bigger than a cat) and weighed 10 kg. As it was a fast runner, this dinosaur could quickly dart away and escape from its predators on its strong back legs.

Big mouthful
Heterodontosaurus (near left) had three types of teeth. The small teeth at the front were used for snipping leaves. Two long fangs were sharp enough to slice through thick stems and may have been used for fighting. The blunter teeth at the back were used for grinding plants.

Scutellosaurus (centre) was a larger relative of Lesothosaurus. It had long arms so probably walked on all-fours. Its body was covered in armour-plating made of bony scales set into the skin, like the scales of a crocodile.

POWERFUL SPRINTERS

A new find

In the Jurassic and Cretaceous Periods
there was a fast-moving
group of plant-eaters called
hypsilophodontids. The best
known is *Hypsilophodon* itself
(front). It lived about 130 million
years ago, was 2 metres long
and weighed about 50 kg.
Hypsilophodon was a typical
fast-running dinosaur.

Gathering evidence

The first *Hypsilophodon* skeleton was found in 1849
in southern England. At first no one was sure how
Hypsilophodon lived. Scientists even wondered if it
perched in trees, like a giant bird. Since then
hypsilophodontid skeletons have been found
all over the world and we know much more
about its lifestyle.

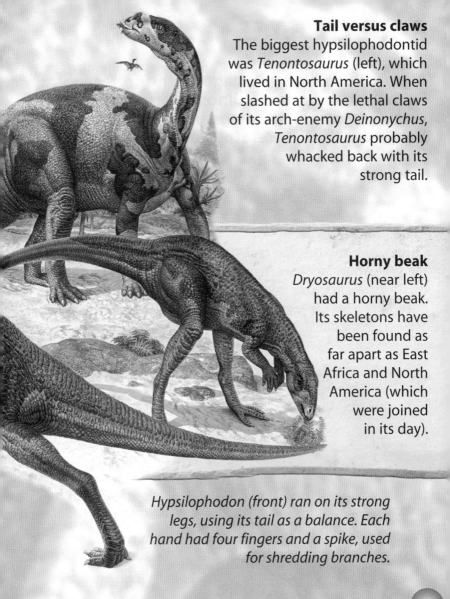

Tail versus claws

The biggest hypsilophodontid was *Tenontosaurus* (left), which lived in North America. When slashed at by the lethal claws of its arch-enemy *Deinonychus*, *Tenontosaurus* probably whacked back with its strong tail.

Horny beak

Dryosaurus (near left) had a horny beak. Its skeletons have been found as far apart as East Africa and North America (which were joined in its day).

Hypsilophodon (front) ran on its strong legs, using its tail as a balance. Each hand had four fingers and a spike, used for shredding branches.

PARROT FACE

About 100 million years ago, in the Cretaceous Period, the horn-faced dinosaurs roamed the Earth. Most were huge, with large bony ruffs and long horns, but the first ceratopsian was quite different.

The first ceratopsian

Psittacosaurus, the first ceratopsian, was much smaller than its later relatives, such as *Triceratops*. Standing up on its hind legs, it was the same size as a human about 1.8 metres and weighed 50 kg. The first specimen was discovered in Mongolia's Gobi Desert in 1922.

Psittacosaurus did not have a horn or a large frill around its head. So what makes it a ceratopsian? The horny part of Psittacosaurus's face is a strange, bony beak, like a parrot's.

Beaky
The beast's massive jaws were worked by strong muscles, so it could eat tough plant food like palm fronds. It stood on its hind legs to reach the trees and pulled down the branches with its hands, eating leaves with its beak.

Tiny baby
Some extremely small baby *Psittacosaurus* skeletons have been found - they are no larger than a pigeon!

BRAINBUSTING QUIZ!

1 **Which was the most fearsome predator of all?**

a) *Tyrannosaurus* b) *Plateosaurus*

2 **What did *Tyrannosaurus* use its very small arms for?**

a) **Putting food in its mouth** b) **No one knows**

3 **How fast did a *Tyrannosaurus* run?**

a) **As fast as a cheetah** b) **It could only walk**

4 **What is a plant-eater called?**

a) **A herbivore** b) **A carnivore**

5 **Why were hadrosaurs called duckbilled dinosaurs?**

a) **Because they had flat mouths like ducks**

b) **Because they swam on a lake**

6 **What were hadrosaur crests used for?**

a) **Snorkels** b) **Making trumpeting calls**

7 **Which dinosaur had a balloon on its forehead?**

a) *Saurolophus* b) *Corythosaurus*

8 **Which dinosaur had the thickest skull of all?**

a) *Pachycephalosaurus* b) *Pinacosaurus*

9 **Why did theropods have backwards-pointing teeth?**

a) **To shred grass** b) **To grip prey**

10 **What does a scavenger eat?**

a) **Dead animal carcasses** b) **Plants**

11 **How can a scientist measure a dinosaur's intelligence?**

a) **By filling its brain cavity with sand, then pouring the sand into a measuring jug**

b) **By counting its teeth**

12 **Which dinosaurs were the most intelligent?**

a) **Troodontids** b) **Dromaeosaurids**